By RUDOLF EUCKEN
Senior Professor of Philosophy in the University of Jena

The Truth of Religion

The Life of the Spirit

Religion and Life

Dr. Rudolf Eucken

Religion and Life

By

Rudolf Eucken

Professor of Philosophy, University of Jena

G. P. Putnam's Sons
New York and London
The Knickerbocker Press
1912

The Knickerbocker Press, New York

PREFACE

THE Lecture, "Religion and Life," by Professor Rudolf Eucken, was delivered in German at Essex Hall, London, on Wednesday, June 7, 1911, and repeated at Manchester College, Oxford, on the following Friday, where it was reported by Mr. Gustav F. Beckh, Ph.D., a student of the College. After the MS. had been corrected by Professor Eucken, the translation was kindly undertaken by Dr. Beckh.

The outline of the Lecture, circulated beforehand, is here reprinted; but Dr.

Eucken departed to some extent from this outline in the actual delivery of his lecture.

The Rev. W. Tudor Jones, Ph.D., contributed the following brief biographical sketch:

"Rudolf Eucken, who visits England for the first time, was born at Aurich, East Friesland, January 5, 1846. He lost his father when quite a child. His mother, a woman of deep religious experience, was the daughter of a Liberal clergyman. At the High School one of the masters—the theologian Reuter—interested him greatly in religion. Religion became of absorbing interest to him when quite a boy; and this interest increased in significance with his classical and philosophical training. He studied at the Universities of Göttingen

Preface

and Berlin. Lotze was Professor of Philosophy at Göttingen and Trendelenburg at Berlin. Trendelenburg influenced him deeply—indeed, settled the direction of his future course in life. After graduating as Doctor of Philosophy at Göttingen, he spent five years as a High School teacher. In 1871, he was appointed Professor of Philosophy at the University of Basel; in 1874, he succeeded Kuno Fischer at Jena. And notwithstanding several calls to larger Universities, it is in the "little nest" of Goethe and Schiller he has chosen to remain. His philosophical works are widely known; his pupils are found from Iceland in the North to New Zealand in the South, from Japan in the East to Britain and America in the West. Those who have had the privilege of knowing him—and his home is always open to his students—are not ever quite the same afterwards and can never forget him.

"In the year 1908, Professor Eucken was awarded the Nobel Prize for Literature. His books have been translated into several European languages; his greatest work—*The Truth of Religion*—has just been published."

Religion and Life

OUTLINE OF THE LECTURE

1. IN placing Religion and Life in close mutual relation we are not concerned with practical and social life, but with life in its broadest sense, including the whole field of science. Our problem is really confined to this, whether in this life it is possible to rise above merely human existence, whether we can discern in it the activity of a Power at once encompassing and transcending the world.

2. This question we answer in the affirmative with entire confidence. When we survey and sum up the traits peculiar

to man, we discover a life essentially different from that of sense; this life we term the life of the Spirit. This spiritual life which manifests itself in the progress of civilisation, is not displayed like the life of Nature in the mutual relations of separate parts; it forms a Whole which is common to us all, and in which we realise our fellowship with others. The life of the soul is in this field not merely a means of physical self-preservation, it gains an independence. The products which it brings forth—Truth, Goodness, Beauty—rise into a realm of inwardness, into a sphere of reality which exists for itself and in itself.

3. This spiritual life with its new contents and relations cannot possibly be a creation of man alone. It must come to

him from the universe; it must form a new stage of reality into which man, who first belongs predominantly to Nature, is raised in the progress of his life. Whatever spiritual energy civilisation displays, receives its genuine content and impelling power only when it is understood as a revelation of an independent spiritual world. At this point, however, we stand if not within the domain of Religion, yet at any rate on its threshold. For henceforth all spiritual creation, all scientific and artistic production, all moral action, appear to be founded in the living presence of a higher Power. With these tasks the individual with his uncertainty and weakness cannot grapple. A higher Power, a power of the Whole, must bear him on, and bring him beyond the gropings of reflection into the security of achievement. Accordingly just on the heights of spiritual production we note a consciousness of dependence and a feeling of deep gratitude. Indeed, the higher the spiritual task which men attempted, the more they felt themselves in labouring at it to be the instruments of a higher Power. We may thus say that all spiritual activity, when traced to its roots and recognised as independent in contrast with petty human aims, develops a kind of religion. This religion which alone imparts a soul to all culture, we may call Universal Religion.

4. But however important it is to discover and recognise in the whole expanse of life a connection with religion, this Uni-

versal Religion is not what is generally understood by Religion. It rather accompanies the general life than constitutes a separate field from which it exerts a peculiar influence. We are thus carried beyond Universal Religion to one that is Characteristic. This is first reached through the experiences, the checks, the shocks, which human life exhibits. Spiritual activity, especially on its moral side, does not advance among us from victory to victory; it encounters the most stubborn resistance, not only from without but in our own soul as well. Such opposition is powerful enough to threaten to bring all life and endeavour to a standstill. In reality, however, life is not cut short by such a check. A new depth is revealed beyond all entanglement, issuing, however, out of an immediate relation of the soul to a life which at once constitutes and transcends the world—only such a life can escape from the world's entanglements. Thus the spiritual life is roused to the conception of Deity, and in developing its relation to the Divine engenders a Characteristic Religion. At the summit of this development the approach of the Deity to man is not limited to occasional points of contact; it makes man a partaker of the fulness of his own life. The union of the Divine and human nature is the fundamental truth of religion, and its deepest mystery consists in the fact that the Divine enters into the compass of the Human without impairing its Divinity. With this new phase life is completely renewed and elevated. Man becomes immediately conscious of the infinite and eternal, of that within him which transcends the world. For the first time the love of God becomes the ruling motive of his life, and brings him into an inner relation with the whole scope of reality. But while this Characteristic Religion unveils new deeps in life, it must still remain within the sphere of human experience, and must in particular seek a friendly union with the Universal Religion. If it cuts itself off and prides itself on being a "specific" religion and evolving a specific piety, it easily sinks into narrowness and rigidity, and is even in danger of pharisaic conceit.

5. Religion thus understood is judged

by the new life which it brings forth. It is the task of thought to make this life clear and set it vividly before our eyes. It cannot, however, produce it by itself. The true demonstration of religion is one of the spirit and of power. The historical religions, however, have their essence in the life peculiar to each, in their unique type of spiritual life. This is what severally distinguishes them, and renders one superior to others. Such life of course needs definite forms. Religion cannot become an historical power and unite men together without forming its own world of ideas, and also without the practice of a cultus which presents the new life to men in visible form. But dogmas and rites have no value except as expressions of the spiritual life of which they are the servants. They must continually be referred back to it or they become lifeless. Further, from this point of view it appears legitimate and indeed necessary, whenever great transformations take place in the world of thought, to exercise an impartial criticism upon them, and reshape them in the interest of the life which they express. Such criticism does not lead to disintegration when it proceeds from the kernel of religion itself instead of from the outside.

6. Such is the situation at the present day. In every field of life penetrating changes have set in, and religion cannot possibly escape them. But while we practise an open and honest criticism on traditional forms, it is needful to develop the

essence of religion the more vigorously. Freedom should not diminish but increase its depth. This, however, will be possible if we bring the new life which unfolds itself in religion, into full action, and transform it into our own life. This will protect us against all paralysing doubt, and give us a sure foothold in the storms of the age. Life and its activity alone can produce a Religion of Life.

RELIGION AND LIFE

New problems are always arising, challenging human endeavour. "Each new morn offers new tasks." Now one of these new tasks undoubtedly is involved in the "Problem of Religion." In years gone by people used to discuss this problem with special reference to the nature of their proofs and the particular ideas contained in them. At the present day we must go to the very root of the problem. The danger has increased. Religion in its entirety is being attacked, and we are compelled to give evidence of its absolute justification and necessity. Various lines have been followed out, and our apology for Religion, I believe, must be based on Life. Life and Religion are things to be defined more closely at the outset. Life, as we take it, means more than practical life. It is more than a mechanical application of laws and doctrines to our daily work. For us, life comprehends every possible kind of activity (including the understanding), superior in its entirety to all its particular branches.

Religion, on the other hand, is not merely a belief in some supreme Power, nor do I consider it to be the establishment of relations of any kind between this supreme Power and ourselves. It is an inner identification with it and the creation of a new life through it. The problem may be therefore defined in this way: Does man in the wholeness of his being experience an impulse to acknowledge a divine element, and if so, can he identify himself with it and rise to its lofty height without transforming his previous condition? And it is to this form of the problem that we must turn our attention first.

Now, even a slight examination of the nature of life will show that it is more than mere existence; that it contains two distinct stages of development.

These stages are—

(a) The stage of natural life.

(b) The stage of spiritual life.

Nobody can deny that to a certain extent we are creatures of nature. It is not only our physical organization that belongs to this department. By means of sensation and impulse nature has a firm hold on our souls as well, and its laws sway our inner life.

In this stage of development there is no inclination towards religion, or towards the creation of an "all-comprehensive" life, controlling, as it were, the world of experience from within. For this natural life is constituted merely of cause and effect, of single organic processes, whose sole purpose it is to exist in opposition to their environments. There is no such thing as a Unity pervading and comprehending the Many, or causing successive experiences to react on each other on the basis of a spiritual principle. All the single elements and processes exist *alongside* of each other, forming a merely *causal* net of relations.

But human life is more than that. We can rise above the limitation of the particular, and can view the "Whole of life." Our mind is fit to deal with humanity at large and with the very infinitude of the universe. The whole of reality is our problem. In this struggle for life man strives after greater things than mere self-preservation. He is capable of establishing a communion with all men and all things. He can place himself in their position. He can find his truest self in others, yea, even in the whole of the universe. The result is an almost instantaneous liberation of his life from the limitation of the particular; he expands and grows above himself.

This progress beyond himself is particularly manifest in the new turn his spiritual life now takes, and in the altered nature of his new problem. In the state of nature, his mental life had been but a means and an instrument of self-preservation. All the cleverness and acuteness of animals serve merely to prolong the existence of individuals, or the whole species, and mental life in this case is but a secondary issue. In man, however, the spiritual life attains to independent existence in the course of his evolution in history. It evolves its own characteristic contents and valuations in the ideas of the True, the Good, and the Beautiful. It expands and becomes a new world within the soul, and in this new world each particular action is inspired by the idea of the whole. This unifying idea of the whole of life may be applied to each particular point of life, and present in it.

Another important distinction ought to be made here: Man in the state of mere nature is but a part of his environment and owes everything to his impressions. In the higher stage, however, he begins to distinguish subject and object, holds them apart, and finally succeeds in transcending this distinction altogether. Science, in a way, accomplishes this transcendence by enabling us to think ourselves into the nature of the object. The work of the artist, his mode of creating things and looking at them, has a similar effect. His work of art represents an inseparable unity of inward soul and outward form, of spiritual and tangible elements. In almost every department we observe this growth of Life, which in its all-comprehensive nature transcends all scattered elements and petty contrasts, and is best defined as "Universal, or Cosmic Life."

We cannot come to realise this, however, without perceiving at the same time that this new turn of development involves a great antinomy, which throws us into almost intolerable difficulties. The new life is there, *in* our souls, but it is, as yet, by no means identical with our being and will. It seems to be produced by us rather than to be a part of ourselves. The natural limitation of man remains, he still is but "a series of single points," and lacks the power to comprehend and explicate this new life. Man proves to be no match for this new task and he cannot attain to this independent "World of the Spirit."

The conditions ensuing from this situation are most disconcerting, as already stated. A merely natural self-preservation does not satisfy him at all. That task he finds to be too small. And yet he cannot rise to the higher stage. The actuating spirit wanes to a shadow without disappearing entirely. Man feels an estrangement towards his inward life. Something separates his present existence from that "mysterious Being." And, what is more fatal still, this conflict produces dualism and ambiguity, which can be traced in the culture and civilisation of all peoples, and which penetrate into the very depth of every human soul. How are we to get out of this conflict?

It is absolutely impossible that man in his limitation should be able to break through this wall of separation. Some higher power must do it for him, and more than that, become part of his own life. It must transfer him into this new world, the Life Universal, and identify his truest self with it. A spiritual life deserving that name is not the activity of a single force but the realisation of Life in its entirety on this particular point of action; it is the tangible experience of being supported and uplifted by this divine power. All productive geniuses have felt that most distinctly. Goethe expresses it in this way: "In artistic production we may collect the fagots and pile them up. But to see them on fire we must wait for the flash of lightning from above."

Great thinkers, in a similar way, have experienced this inward necessity, whenever they opposed the current opinions of their time. A statesman like Gladstone, for example, once said he could easily conceive of *theoretical* doubts of the existence of a higher Being, but a statesman, standing at the helm, certainly could never experience such doubts. For without this consciousness of being led by a higher Power, the innumerable responsibilities of his position would be more than human nature could bear.

But as soon as man acknowledges the

manifestation of this divine element and participates in this new creation through divine power and grace, life will be altogether transformed. Now at last we are standing in the great river of Life, of which we were allowed to touch no more than the brink in our first stage of development; it is here that we find a new self, our true Spiritual Life. The cleavage in the depth of our souls is bridged over at last. That inner estrangement, so often felt, has disappeared and the whole universe is now part of regenerate man's experience. Now we may justly say, "All things are yours, but ye are God's." Now true love may be developed and the joys of life experienced to their fullest extent. That feeling of isolation disappears, which has so often depressed us, and we are conscious of partaking in that "inner life" common to all of us. And this autonomous creation of a true spiritual life is the great wonder, and the only certain evidence on behalf of religion.

This kind of religion, the source of all spiritual life, we may venture to call "Universal Religion."

Without this Religion no true civilisation is possible. A civilisation declining all contact with a supernatural life and refusing to establish those mysterious "inner relations" gradually degenerates into a mere human civilisation, and becomes a *Kultur komödie* (parody of civilisation), as Pestalozzi has called it.

The life of every individual person is

affected by this "Problem of Religion." I cannot conceive of the development of a powerful personality, a deep-rooted and profound mind, or a character rising above this world, without his having experienced this divine life. And as surely as we can create in ourselves a life in contrast to pure nature, growing by degrees and extending to the heights of the True, the Good, and the Beautiful, we may have the same assurance of that religion called Universal.

But this great turning-point in our development naturally brings us into contact with new difficulties and grave problems. We expect from a religious point of view that the Divine element should be omnipotent in this world, that it should expel the powers of darkness, accomplish the definite victory of good over evil, and turn this world of sensible reality into a world of reason. This is by no means the case. Our experience soon tells us that sorrow and suffering, weakness and wickedness, are still all-powerful. For nature seems to take little notice of our spiritual interests and purposes: earthquakes, floods, and tempests are continually nipping the buds of life, and we are every one of us exposed to these crude powers of destruction. Of a still graver nature are the antinomies of our inner life. "The Good" fails to predominate in human nature, spiritual powers are employed for very unspiritual ends, and a kind of egotism arises, such as the world has never seen before, opposing the whole of life and making it a means to an end rather than an end in itself; an egotism which delights in opposing "the Good," and warring against the Divine element. How will our universal religion fit in with this power of evil? Are we not inevitably led to doubt the power and reality of the Divine?

This problem has occupied man's mind for thousands of years, and continually disturbed and harassed it. Many solutions have been attempted, of which the following are more or less typical. *Optimism* tries to explain away evil by adopting a standard of criticism broad enough even to allow the power of evil as being in harmony with a higher order of the universe. But this solution of the problem of evil is impossible for the simple reason that we are not merely reflective, but sensitive and active beings in this world-process, and therefore cannot simply "reason" sufferings out of the way.

Stoicism is another of these typical attempts. It found the purpose and greatness of life in keeping suffering and passion at a distance, and by crushing the emotional side of our nature. Fate has placed us in this or that dangerous and exposed position. In spite of the darkness around us we are to persevere like brave soldiers. Alas, by crushing the emotional side, the virtues of love and charity were exiled and an isolation of the soul ensued. Besides, to persevere in the battle of life is no satisfactory ideal of life. We must know for what the battle is fought, to what results it will lead, and whether we shall achieve "new things."

Another typical solution, and to my mind the only remaining one, lies in the narrowing down of "Universal Religion" to "Characteristic Religion."

By *"Characteristic Religion"* I mean a religion which allows of conflict, suffering, and sin, as opening new doors, leading into greater depths, and creating a life of pure "inwardness," a life drawing its strength from the relation of an individual soul to the "Spring of all Life."

It is often said that "Suffering makes a man better and refines his nature." But that is not the inevitable consequence. Experience proves that people often become narrow, petty, and envious through suffering.

Sorrow in itself does not help man; but under its stress we *may* develop and gain a new life, which *may* mean the opening up of a divine life, given by the grace of a divine power outside of us, creating *in* us a new centre of spiritual life, lifting us above material toil, and imbuing us with an inward power transcending the world of things.

We Germans have the proverb, "A man is worth more than his work." This "more," however, is only attained by means of a Characteristic Religion. On that basis we can understand the great saying of Jesus, "What shall a man be profited, if he gain the whole world and forfeit his soul?"

I have not claimed that in this discovery of the new depths of life our old conflicts and antinomies disappear. Darkness there still is; but our struggle is not in vain, if we gain a new life through it, and are born a second time. This struggle through harsh negation to a cheerful "yea," this ascent above our suffering through acknowledging it, is the fundamental truth of Christianity as I understand it. Through developing this idea and working it out fully it has attained its peculiar characteristics. Only on the basis of this conception could it make the cross its symbol and carry it victoriously through the world. This fundamental truth is beautifully expressed by the greatest German poet:

"Those who have not understood
'Die, and rise to-morrow!'
They are but as passing shades
In this world of sorrow."

And Luther powerfully puts it thus: "That I call spiritual power, which can remain erect in the midst of our enemies and show its strength in a state of humiliation. And its very essence is strength in weakness, enabling us to gain salvation in all conditions, and compelling death, yea, even the cross, to further our salvation and yield life."

That is what I believe to be the character of Christianity. It is the preservation of life in sharpest contradiction with the world. It is a triumphant progress to cheerful affirmation in spite of the spirit of negation. It is the inward extinction of sorrow through the creation of a higher life, and persists in growing through all the turmoil of strife and suffering. Human life may thus be said to set itself a noble task and to develop spiritually.

Now at last a true "world-history" begins, for every individual soul can now make its own history. Classical literature in all its variety and profound value contains not *one* "history of a soul." The memoirs of Marcus Aurelius, though full of noble reflections, contain no such testimony. It is the imperishable merit of St. Augustine to have written the first literary biography of a soul in his *Confessions*. Such a biography could only be of value and interest in a time when people began to hold with Luther "that not for the price of the whole world may we lose one single soul, however humble."

This new life with all its contrasts and rich inner developments in spite of all external vexation, cannot be described adequately in words. The artist must do that for us, the religious poet, and especially the composer of sacred music, of music like that of Bach and Handel. But this acquisition is of "world-historical" importance, creating a spiritual reality never dreamt of before, and proving Christianity to be the religion of all religions in the past history of this world. Not that we understand things better now. The elements of darkness may be as prevalent as ever. But with darkness we have gained depth, and there are events in our soul's life at present which leave no doubt as to the course of the future.

Fundamental truths, however, standing above the change of time, are constantly present "monitors." As soon as Religion means the sounding of new depths and the production of a new reality, we have passed beyond the sphere of Intellectualism, which would fain make religion a cosmology. But we are just as unwilling to make religion a purely emotional matter, rejecting the undeniable realities of human existence and giving full sway to subjectivism. True religion, with its new reality, must form a characteristic sphere of life for itself and produce a characteristic community of men, seeking its most active realization in the very establishment of this community. And here again we meet with new conflicts arising out of the relations between Divine and human elements. Certainly the new life is altogether a gift of God. The Divine does not conform and adapt itself to human standards. All human "littleness" is broken up in the process of regeneration; man is received into the fulness of divine life and partakes of its infinitude. But all the same, the formation of the new life cannot take place without human endeavour, and this power is roused in the struggle of life. I admit that man can never express the Divine adequately. "All passing things are but symbols" (Goethe's *Faust*) is a truth for all times. We cannot get beyond the *quest* and *search* for truth. We may demand, however, that the Divine should be expressed in the relatively highest forms, that we should always try to find the most adequate symbol.

Thus we may account for changes and varieties, and it may be that the process of human history renders certain symbols inadequate, which in times past were considered perfect. But as soon as we become aware of such a cleavage between the essence of Religion and its latest rendering in symbol, it is our most sacred duty to bridge it over and provide a more adequate rendering.

No doubt we are aware of such a cleavage at the present day. In order to preserve Christianity in all its strength and beauty we must find new forms and symbols for it. For since it first came into existence and received its traditional form, a tremendous change has taken place. Our world is larger than the world of those days, with regard to our conceptions of nature as well as those of human history. Many forms are now but anthropomorphisms which two thousand years ago satisfied the very best of minds. And what was considered in those times to be a pure expression or reflection of the Divine in Christianity, is now verging dangerously near the mythological element. Let us not forget that Christianity entered into history at a time when the old world was in a state of resignation and degeneration, when people took the sorrows and evils of their days as a kind of inevitable destiny. This is vividly illustrated by the fact that nobody ventured to combat the irrationality of their social conditions, such as poverty and slavery, and that their morality was of a purely passive nature.

Our age, however, has inspired us with wonderful self-confidence and manly vigour. We are convinced that there are great possibilities in man. We are challenged to throw in the whole of our strength and labour in uprooting misery and want. We desire to make human life more rational. And in the organisation of religious and devotional life we must needs demand more individual liberty and greater possibilities of free development than the ancients required. They thought but little of the strength of individuals and attempted chiefly to create a powerful organisation and authority, taking all responsibility from the shoulders of the individual and preserving him from all manner of doubt and uncertainty. And, finally, we are no longer satisfied with a traditional cult embodying the Divine in more or less tangible forms. The ideas of spiritual and material, of supernatural and physical, were not held apart in ancient minds with the precision of to-day. They believed that the Divine must needs manifest himself in tangible matter, as the early teachings of the Eucharist show. We are poignantly conscious of the irremediable contrast between Spirit and Matter and resent the magical element, which seems to us to impair the purely religious. Purely religious it was to *them*. But we are inevitably confronted with new problems, which can only be solved in a state of liberty, of absolute freedom for all minds.

In taking up the task of remodelling Christianity (*merely* in its *forms*) we are acting on behalf of Religion. We are not criticising for the sake of criticism, but are longing to come to an everlasting "yea." We do not want less, but more of religion. New social problems are awaiting their solution. Serious inroads are made on Christianity and what is of still graver importance, the whole of our people are making them. And I assure you that Christianity can only grapple with these difficulties by absorbing and employing *all* the results and fruits of the "world-historical" work of humanity at large. And its best contents, its very life-blood, can only become a possession of the civilised world if it adapts its forms and symbols to the conditions of our time. It must become *altogether* a religion of the moving and flowing present. Nothing obsolete and antique can be allowed to remain in it, and it must unite and focus all our modern intellectual and spiritual aspirations. It must excise all the pusillanimous and petty elements of man's nature. In this reforming process we must carefully avoid putting our modern interpretation into old things. That leads to unhealthy results and runs counter to the saying of the greatest of the Greek Fathers: "In the soul of a truly religious man all elements must be absolutely genuine."

Those standing at a greater distance may object to this spiritualisation of religion, as being nothing more than a process of dilution and evaporation, at any rate a surrender of the best. But may I be allowed to say that every single attempt in history to reform religion and spiritualise the symbols, by rejecting its more tangible elements, has been regarded by the adherents of sacred tradition as a perilous process of dissolution. The early Christians were called Atheists because they rejected all images of their godhead, and at the present day Catholics believe that the Protestant religion sadly lacks tangible elements of worship.

Religion and Life 43

But as a matter of fact Reality is to be found not outside of the world of the Spirit, but *in* it. And the sooner we become aware of this in religion, and the sooner it seeks contact with the whole of life, casting its anchor in the harbour of life, the sooner will it appeal to humanity and counteract the workings of scepticism.

Is it not true that *we* particularly want a religion fresh and new-born, bringing forth fruit of all kinds? I admit that the waters of the surface are all against religion. But the undercurrent of man's soul is all in its favour. Modern culture has succeeded on many lines. But it has also given us many a grave problem, for which it is no match.

This yearning and craving amid the

unwholesomeness of a secular, merely human culture, this intolerable shallowness of life, which cannot reach beyond its circuit, all the folly and madness of purely human activities and aims, this rush to and fro, without love and without soul—how do you account for them? And on the other side the *profound longing* for greater depths, for greater stability and permanence! This yearning to partake of a *higher* life than that which the process of natural and social self-preservation will allow us! Believe me, this incessantly growing impulse, running through all nations and all civilisations of the East and West, is in itself a proof that powers are at work in our souls, of which our critics will have to give account. Pascal justly remarked: "You would not have sought me, had I not been there already."

Of course, we are fully aware of the fact that we are seekers, that our achievements are not perfect yet. But we are convinced at the same time that we are serving a great end, which is not the creation of our own brains, but set up for us in the process of evolution.

And as to the attempt to reform Christian truths, and clothe them in new symbols, let us remember what the wise Gamaliel said (Acts v: 38, 39): "And now I say unto you, Refrain from these men, and let them alone; for if this counsel or this work be of men, it will be overthrown; but if it is of God, ye will not be able to overthrow them; lest haply ye be found even to be fighting against God."

Let us therefore work cheerfully, every man in his own place and way; all, however, supported by the firm conviction that we are partakers of the work of the Spirit, and that nothing can be in vain, if it has been done with a view to our great end and in the faithful fulfilment of our task.

*A Selection from the
Catalogue of*

G. P. PUTNAM'S SONS

**Complete Catalogue sent
on application**

By Rudolf Eucken
Awarded Noble Prize, 1908
Senior Professor of Philosophy in the University of Jena

The Truth of Religion

Translated by W. Tudor Jones, Ph.D.

Theological Translation Library, New Series
Octavo. $3.00 net. By mail, $3.25

It is written in an inquiring spirit to elucidate the problem of religion in its relation to all the most distinctive features of our modern-day life. The book is addressed "to all those," to quote Eucken's own words, "who, like myself, feel that they cannot endure any longer the shallows in which the vitality of man's spirit is being lost at present, and who are determined, in spite of all that is superficial in contemporary life, to share the quest for deepening and revival." The book is divided into five parts, the headings of which are: First, introductory; second, the fundamental basis of the universal religion; third, the opposition to religion; fourth, the religion that is religious; fifth, Christianity and modern life.

The Life of the Spirit
An Introduction to Philosophy

Translated by F. L. Pogson, M.A.

Second Edition with Introductory Note by the Author.
Second Impression. Crown Theological Library.
Cr. 8vo. $1.50 net. By mail, $1.65

Professor Eucken's philosophy is a philosophy of life. It is a philosophy of reality as well. It treats of the sources of man's strength, and the meaning and purpose of his spiritual endeavor. And can there be anything more real than the activity of a life that has consciously realized the true sources of its power and the goal of its ultimate aspiration?

| New York | **G. P. Putnam's Sons** | London |

Crown Theological Library

This series has been instituted to present a religious literature dealing with modern difficulties; the thinking man needs books on a subject so vital as that of religious thought, which take into account all that is most valuable and trustworthy in modern research. The volumes comprising the "Crown Theological Library" have been selected with a view of meeting the religious questionings of the present age, and each contribution has been prepared by an acknowledged authority on the subject with which it deals. The standpoint of the series is at once reverent and liberal. Its object is to combine respect for religion with respect for historic and scientific truth, and to present a series of studies on the great problems of human life which are free from all dogmatic prepossessions.

Volumes range in price from $1.25 net to $1.75 net

Complete list of titles sent upon application

G. P. Putnam's Sons
New York   London